P9-DYX-826

# let's travel in

# CHINA

Edited by Darlene Geis

A TRAVEL PRESS BOOK

PICTURE ACKNOWLEDGMENTS
The illustrations in this book are the work of the following photographers and artists, whose collaboration is gratefully acknowledged. For the full-color pictures, The Globe and Mail, Toronto, P.I.P. (2, 3, 4, 5, 6, 8, 9, 10, 12, 14, 15, 17, 18, 22, 27, 30, 31, 32); Brian Brake, from Magnum (1, 21, 23); Marc Riboud, from Magnum (11, 20, 24, 26); Ewing Krainin (28); Three Lions (29). For the black-and-white photographs we wish to thank Marc Riboud and Brian Brake from Magnum; and Three Lions. The map was made by Emerson Barron (Mann Associates).

Original copyright, © 1962 by Columbia Record Club, New York, N. Y. under the title of *A Colorslide Tour of China*. All rights reserved.
New edition published 1965 by CHILDRENS PRESS, INC., Chicago.
Published simultaneously in Canada.              Lithographed in the U.S.A.
Library of Congress Catalog Card Number: 65-12225

# CONTENTS

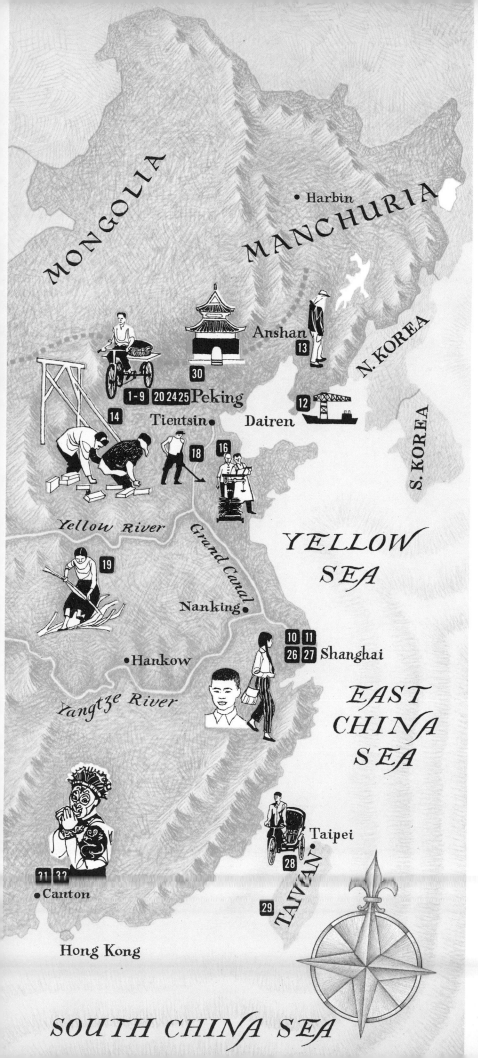

# Locales of thirty-two full-page pictures

# CHINA, GIANT OF THE EAST

TO TRAVEL to China is, for most Westerners, a bewildering experience. You step across the border into a world in which the speech and clothes, the writing, the architecture, the very way in which people think and feel, appear utterly strange. Many of the customs will seem topsy-turvy. Soup comes at the end of the meal, writing is still often up and down, white is the color of mourning and sadness. You will find the Chinese laughing at things we would not consider funny at all, and at other times you will see them become impassive when we would laugh. Their music, melodious to them, sounds shrill and harsh to us; and though their manners are delicate and their behavior restrained they seem to be able to stand more sheer noise than any other people.

China is the oldest country in the world. For over three thousand years she has enjoyed an unbroken continuity of cultural tradition. She was a well-established country before the founding of Rome. During the Middle Ages the upper classes of China possessed a standard of cultural refinement never before equaled in the world, and at that time the population of China was probably greater than the population of all the rest of the world combined.

It is inevitable that Chinese customs and ways seem so alien, for her civilization developed with almost no contact with Europe. Occasional travelers, like Marco Polo, would return to Europe with stories of a fabulous empire in the East, but for centuries there was virtually no exchange of ideas or commerce between China and Europe.

Indeed, China did all she could to resist Western influence. With a superb arrogance and a profound ignorance of the rest of the world, the Chinese felt that they could continue to live on as they were indefinitely, uncorrupted by contact with others. But in the nineteenth century, when China was confronted with the military strength of the Western powers, her essential weakness was revealed. Tradition was no match for technology. The ancient culture crumbled under the impact of Western power and Western ideas, and the country became divided into warring factions. Weak, unable to resist invasion, ill-governed, the ordinary people of China gradually sank to depths of indescribable poverty and degradation, which all the help of America and other countries could do little to mitigate. Yet there remained, deep in the consciousness of the Chinese people, a conviction of their innate superiority. Culturally they continued to look upon us as barbarians.

This deep disdain for the West, this certainty of China's moral position has, even at the best of times, made her a difficult country to deal with.

## CHINA'S CONTRIBUTIONS TO MANKIND

During the long centuries before the West made contact, China's art was unsurpassed. Her writers, her philosophers, her poets still speak to us across the years. For the peoples of the Far East, China played the role that Greece and Rome played for Europe and the Western world, contributing systems of law, government and philosophy to many other nations.

From the twenty-second century before Christ, when China was governed by the first of her twenty-four dynasties, she was self-sufficient until the modern era. By the sixth century B.C. China had developed a written language capable of expressing the most subtle ranges of human thought. Confucius (*kon-*FEW-*shus*) and Lao-tzu (*lah-oo-tsuh*) each inspired a system of philosophy and ethics which, with Buddhism, form the major religious influences to this day.

*This pottery horse was made more than a thousand years ago during the T'ang dynasty, China's golden age of art.*

It is not only in the field of art and philosophy that the Chinese have contributed to the general store of human wisdom. They were the first to make porcelain (we still call our cups and plates "china"). Chinese mariners invented the compass. It was in China that printing was invented, and paper and gunpowder. Among the strange "new" objects that Marco Polo brought back to his native Italy from China were coal and, oddly enough, noodles and ravioli, which the Italians have adopted as their own national dishes.

## THE VASTNESS OF CHINA

After Russia and Canada, China is the largest country in the world. Excluding the island of Taiwan (*tie-wahn*), also known as Formosa, the area is 3,745,000 square miles—somewhat larger than the United States. Her border is more than 16,000 miles long, and the peasants of the western province of Sinkiang (*sin-chee-ahng*) are finishing breakfast at seven o'clock when the citizens of Harbin (HAHR-*bin*) in the northeast are sitting down to their midday meal.

According to Chinese mythology the topography of China was

10

determined more than five thousand years ago by a giant named Pan Goo. With his chisel and hammer, he shattered the solid rock which covered the globe. He stacked the rubble in piles beyond the plains of China, thus forming the Himalaya, and then—worn out by this arduous task—he lay down and died.

Whatever one may think of this story of Pan Goo, it gives us a picture of China sloping from the great heights of the Himalayan range eastward to the sea. All the principal rivers flow from west to east. One of China's most famous rivers is the Yangtze (YAHNG-*tsuh*), or Ocean's Son—the world's fourth-longest river—which flows for over three thousand miles on its path to the Pacific Ocean, dividing northern from southern China. Its gorges in Szechwan (*suh-chwahn*) province are famous for their spectacular beauty. Another great river of China is the Hwang Ho (*hwahng hoh*), or Yellow River. Year after year, hundreds of thousands were drowned and millions made homeless when the Hwang Ho overflowed its banks, and it became known as "China's Sorrow." One of the first major tasks that the Communist government tackled was the taming of this river, and today, visitors are almost certain to be urged to see its huge dams and hydroelectric projects.

With all the rivers flowing from west to east, there was no transport link from north to south until the Grand Canal was dug between the Yangtze and the Hwang Ho. It is the world's longest canal, measuring more than a thousand miles; and we have a startling picture of China's great past when we learn that ships were plying the Grand Canal four hundred years before the Christian era.

Rice, the most important crop in the land, is raised throughout central and south China. In the north the staple foods are wheat, millets and beans. Tropical fruit, like bananas, pineapples, oranges and peaches, grows in the south. In the north, where rivers and lakes remain frozen for three months or more a year, apples and pears thrive.

## ONE FOURTH OF MANKIND

With nearly 700 million inhabitants, China has a population greater than that of the United States, the Soviet Union and Western Europe combined. And the population is growing by more than fifteen hundred *every hour*. Since you picked up this book five minutes ago, the population of China has increased by a hundred and twenty-five.

The need to feed, clothe and find work for a quarter of the human race is a problem that must haunt any Chinese government. It is the one problem that dominates all others. In an attempt to give equal shares of what there is available, food, cloth and other supplies are strictly rationed. So huge is the population that to allow the use of a single yard

11

more cloth per year by each Chinese would wipe out the surplus that China now sells abroad. Every morning ninety million Chinese children go off to primary school—and books and pencils and desks have to be provided for them. An official in the Department of Health in Peking will describe the astonishing problems they were confronted with when, in a drive for the better care of teeth, they found that nylon factories had to be constructed because there could never be enough natural bristles to make toothbrushes in such colossal quantities!

## MODERN CHINA

The history of modern China began in 1911 with the overthrow of the Manchu dynasty and the birth of the Chinese Republic under the late Sun Yat-sen (*soon yaht-sen*), who is still respected by Nationalists and Communists alike as the George Washington of China. For almost forty years, however, China continued to suffer the ravages of warlords, Japanese invasion and civil war.

In the mid-Twenties, two rival factions, the Chinese Nationalists or Kuomintang (*kwoh-min-dong*), and the Chinese Communists or Goon-changdong (*goon-chahng-dong*), began a long, bitter struggle for supremacy. From 1928 until the end of World War II, the Nationalists kept the Communists in check, while they also fought the Japanese.

Following the defeat of the Japanese, the civil war in China flared up anew. The small band of soldiers fighting with Mao Tse-tung (*mah-oo tsuh-toong*) had grown into a formidable army, and with runaway inflation, hardship and growing discontent of the people, the Nationalists were fighting a losing battle. In 1949 the Nationalists, led by Chiang Kai-shek (*chee-ahng kigh-shek*), retreated to the island of Taiwan about a hundred miles off the China coast. Since that time China has been divided into two entities. There is the Nationalist Republic of China on Taiwan, with a population of about 10,000,000 people. And on October 1, 1949, the Communists, then in control of mainland China, established a new government, the People's Republic of China, in the capital of Peking. A new chapter in the long story of China had begun.

## CHINA UNDER THE COMMUNISTS

The Communists moved swiftly to gain as much popular support as possible. They confiscated all land and distributed it to nearly 400 million peasants. The new government established a health program, a public educational system; it gave equal rights to women and abolished the old feudal marriage system; and it gave top priority to the building of heavy industrial plants.

But as we travel through the country by train or riverboat, we discover

12

that over four-fifths of China's people live off the land. And—as was the case in Russia after the revolution there—it is agriculture that is the weak link. Since 1950, farming in China has undergone three major changes. The first was "land reform"—which gave small plots of land to millions of tenant farmers. The government quickly realized that this was no solution. The second phase was the co-operatives, in which all the land, animals and implements were owned in common by the members, with each peasant's income depending on the amount of work he contributed. The third phase was the establishment of the communes. They were created by merging several co-operatives and local administrative units into a single organization which would be responsible not only for agriculture but for small industry, education, roads, health, and all the other functions formerly carried out by local administrations.

*Food and education are two of China's biggest problems. Young and old must study after the day's work.*

Of all the steps taken by Red China, the establishment of the communes in 1958, according to many reports, is the harshest blow to any hope of future freedom for the peasants. That it has caused intense hardship cannot be questioned—and this is proved by the refugees who choose to leave their homes for a precarious but free existence in Hong Kong.

## TRAVELING IN CHINA

The traveler in China will find many curious and puzzling contradictions. Despite the immense changes of the past ten years, we discover that the old temples, the palaces, the ancient shrines are being carefully restored and beautifully maintained.

The Westerner, expecting to find the appalling dirt and squalor of many Asian countries, will be surprised by how clean China is—at least in the large cities. Immense efforts have been made to teach the Chinese the basic principles of public health. Those with colds are expected to wear a surgical mask; the water in the big cities is now safe to drink; modern sewage systems have made the fearful smells of the Chinese cities a thing of the past.

The last decade has seen a new China emerge. Yet in some ways this ancient land is unchanged. It retains much of its rare charm and immense physical beauty. No one can travel in China without becoming aware that he is among people with ancient traditions but determined to move forward as fast as possible into the twentieth century. What this portends no one yet can tell, but as we start our tour we inevitably recall the prophetic words uttered by Napoleon a hundred and fifty years ago: "China? There lies a sleeping giant. Let him sleep, for when he wakes he will move the world."

*In rural China many of the old ways remain, though elsewhere family life is fast disappearing.*

# let's travel in

# CHINA

# TEMPLE
# OF HEAVEN:
# PEKING
# LANDMARK

THE ancient and imperial city of Peking has existed under one name or another since the twelfth century B. C. It has seen great dynasties flourish and decay, it has known Tatar and Mongol masters and in this century it was in Japanese hands for eight years. Now Peking is the capital of Red China, but the old splendor of the Chinese emperors outshines the modern aspects of the city.

Here a group of kindergarten tots are visiting one of the marvels of the past with their teacher. Six hundred years ago this enormous Temple of Heaven was erected on a broad compound in the southern part of Peking. Rising from a marble terrace the three-tiered shrine, with its blue tile roofs glinting in the sun, is one of the most perfectly proportioned buildings in the world.

In the years before the Chinese Republic this was the scene of one of the great imperial ceremonies. Each spring the emperor and his court left the walled Forbidden City and came to this shrine, also known as the Hall of Annual Prayer for Good Crops. The emperor and his retinue were clothed in magnificent blue robes, and as they made their way across this terrace the sight must have been a stirring one. Inside the temple the emperor offered sacrifices and prayed for rich harvests. Then as now, food for China's millions was a problem that seriously concerned the country's leaders.

In 1889 flames destroyed much of the Temple of Heaven. When it was rebuilt, the new pillars supporting the roof were made of Oregon pine. It is kept in good repair today, and there are usually throngs of people who come to admire one of Peking's most exquisite buildings. Children clamber up and down the terraces, and there are stalls where souvenirs and candy are sold. One wonders whether a few surreptitious prayers for good crops are ever whispered here nowadays.

16

# NORTH SEA PARK: AN EMPEROR'S GARDEN

PEKING, which means "Northern Capital," commands the passes to the Mongolian plateau, from which Mongol horsemen used to charge down in periodic raids. The Great Wall of China was built as protection against them and on a clear day you can see it from Peking. The city itself has walls within walls, and here, inside the central Imperial City, are the elaborate gardens, pavilions and lakes that were built for an emperor's delight. The buildings are charming to look at, but when you hear their names you are enchanted by the romance of old Cathay—Pavilion of Darting Fish, Kiosk of Clouds Reflected in the Waters, Hall of Beautiful Waves.

The great Kublai Khan, China's Mongol emperor in the thirteenth century, made Peking his capital. It was here that the dazzled Marco Polo stayed for many years. When he returned to his native Venice he was branded as the liar of all time for the tales he told of this magnificent city where people burned rocks (coal) and used money made of paper! None of Kublai Khan's stately pleasure domes remain, but one of his palaces stood here where a later emperor created these fabulous gardens.

The marble bridge in this picture spans an artificial lake called the North Sea. In the days of the Manchu rulers, water pageants with mock naval battles were held on the sea, and in the winter, when the water was frozen, members of the court, dressed in sumptuous furs and silks, would glide over the ice on skates. Today the formal gardens are a public park. We see North Sea Park on an early winter's day when the city is swept by the cold winds from Siberia. But winter or summer the citizens of Peking enjoy their parks. In this weather, young and old will make tracks for the frozen lake with their skates. In summer the same lake is dotted with hundreds of gaily colored rowboats. The delightful gardens of long ago are still fulfilling their original function and giving people pleasure.

# IMPERIAL LION: GUARDIAN OF THE GATE

**T**HE Chinese, ever proud of their long past, have recently restored many of their old buildings and monuments with great skill and care. Here we have penetrated to the very heart of Peking—to a walled rectangle within the Imperial City, the innermost sanctum that was known as the Forbidden City. Court functionaries lived in the Imperial City, but the Forbidden City was the home of the god-emperors, where few persons not of royal blood could ever set foot. Within this moated red-walled area all the mystery and intrigue that surrounded the Dragon Throne of the Ming and Manchu emperors took place.

Although the dragon is the traditional emblem of China, the lion was the symbol of the emperor's power on earth. The great Golden Lion here stands guard at one of the entrances to the Imperial Palace. Lions, always in pairs, indicate the grounds and buildings that were exclusively the emperor's. The male lion holds a ball beneath his paw, the lioness fondles a cub. The public is now admitted to the rooms where emperors once lived in splendid seclusion, and today people calmly walk past these guardians of a vanished power.

*The Forbidden City, behind its sentinel lions, is open to the public now.*

# MARBLE BOAT: THE SUMMER PALACE

THIS marble boat was the whim of one of China's last Manchu rulers, the Empress Dowager Tz'ŭ Hsi (*tsoo shee*), who died in 1908. Nicknamed "the old Buddha," this strong-minded and stubborn woman kept her nephew, the rightful emperor, in prison for a long time while she ran the country. Under seventeenth-century Manchu rulers China had reached the highest point in her history, but by the end of the nineteenth century the Manchus had become wasteful and decadent, and the people were growing rebellious.

The Empress Dowager took an enormous fund of money that had been raised to build a Chinese navy, and she lavished it on her Summer Palace instead. The Marble Boat is the only vessel China ever got from these naval appropriations. The Summer Palace became the old Empress's favorite residence, and it is on this boat that she used to sit sipping tea while watching the sun set beyond the western hills.

She also had a theater with three stages set one above the other. When the mood seized her, she would get up and act on one of them. Otherwise there were three plays going at once, and the Empress could sit back and watch whichever one she preferred.

The Empress Dowager bent the world to her iron will, and anything she didn't like she changed. She was bitterly opposed to foreign influence, which was increasing in China, and in the Boxer Rebellion she encouraged her militia to massacre all foreigners. On a more harmless level, the old Buddha decided to change the topography of Peking, which was too flat for her taste. She had a large lake excavated, and then piled all the soil up around it in a series of artificial hills. In this manufactured setting she placed her "marble folly," the boat we see here. It is an eloquent example of the Court's isolation from the realities of the times, and from the hungry, teeming life of the ordinary Chinese. And it gives us a clue to at least one of the causes of the overthrow of the Manchus and the forming of a republic.

# PEKING:
# THE OLD AND
# THE NEW

HERE is one of the streets of the capital on a crisp, clear autumn afternoon. Peking is a city in which horse carts are still seen, as well as modern trucks. In no other city in the world, not even Rome or Athens, does a traveler feel so powerfully the sense of age, the continuity of history. Peking, like ancient Rome, was one of the few cities to reach a million inhabitants long before the industrial age. Today it is a rapidly developing industrial city with a population of over four million.

Like so much else in China, Peking is a curious mixture of the old and the new. Light-blue electric trolley buses glide along modern boulevards, but not far off there may be an intricate maze of little lanes which have not changed much in hundreds of years. Many of the streets still retain their old poetic names—Fire Genie Street, Jade Street, The Street of Beautiful Objects, Embroidery Street.

The beautiful objects for which China was famous are no longer being made, though there are still merchants who have a small stock remaining from former times, which they sell to tourists. Each large city has at least one state-owned department store, where the city dwellers (whose income is much higher than that of the peasants) can find the sheer necessities of life. But such things as perfumes, fancy soaps and (though this is still rare) even lipstick are the only luxuries on sale.

*The gorgeous silks of old China have been replaced by cotton cloth, sturdy and practical.*

25

# TIEN AN MEN: CHINA'S "RED SQUARE"

WE ARE now in the very center of Peking's ancient magnificence. This is Tien An Men (*tyen ahn men*), which means "Gate of Heavenly Peace." Built in 1651 by the first Manchu emperor, it was the main entrance to the Imperial City, the ceremonial gateway through which the emperors of China were carried on state occasions. The Communist government has recently enlarged the square that lies before this gate. It is now five times larger than St. Peter's Square in Rome, which is Europe's largest. Tien An Men is today the symbolic heart of the new China, and it is here that all the largest rallies and parades are held. It is ironic that this violently anti-imperialistic regime should choose to have its most important rallying ground in the shadow of the Imperial City.

Tien An Men, despite its serene name, has had a violent history. It was partly destroyed on several occasions and has been the scene of many bitter struggles. In this century, during the turbulent political conflicts of the Twenties and Thirties, Tien An Men became the traditional protest ground for demonstrating students. More than once police have fired on the crowds here, leaving many dead.

Tien An Men is a building of extraordinary beauty, combining massive strength with an exquisite grace. Its curved roofs of golden tile appear to brood over the city of Peking, and even the huge slogan on the wall, written in the ancient and graceful characters, seems to have a poetic beauty. For those who read Chinese, however, the sentiment is lacking in the usual delicate subtlety of this land. "Long Live the Unity of the People's Republic," it says.

26

# CHINESE MAY DAY: WORKERS' HOLIDAY

PARADES have become an important feature of life in Red China. The Chinese people have always loved shows of all kinds, from the five-hour-long Peking Opera to the village storyteller. Under their present government the Chinese are extremely well-organized, and on a holiday like May Day, or National Day which comes on October 1st, the people get a chance to put on a theatrical display of staggering proportions.

Staged in the enormous Tien An Men Square, the parade involves thousands of people from all walks of life. The nation's leaders are assembled on a long gallery that runs the length of the red-walled gate. Before them pass file after file of people, all of whom have been specially chosen and trained for the honor of marching in this show. There are peasants who carry exhibits of their crops or the animals they raise; members of the national minorities—Tibetans, Mongolians, people of Sinkiang, and Moslems; athletes like the ones in this picture holding up their red banners against the spring sky; acrobats; women's army groups; actors, dancers and students. For these few hours bright colors flood the streets of Peking, balloons soar into the air and regimentation puts on its gayest face.

*Fireworks, an invention of the ancient Chinese, illuminate the vast square and Great Hall of the People.*

# MEN AND ANIMALS: THEY ALL WORK

FROM the organized gaiety of a holiday parade we return to the hard realities of life in China today. Yet, even as we uncomfortably watch this wagon being drawn by both men and animals, we realize that just around the corner there may be an electronics plant as modern as anything in the Western world. The Chinese say this is "walking on two legs"—using both old and new methods to get ahead.

Wherever we go in China, whatever we see, we realize that this is a country with one foot in the Middle Ages and the other in the twentieth century. While old Chinese doctors still practice the traditional "acupuncture" (in which long silver needles are driven deep into the flesh), some of the younger doctors are operating in hospitals with the most up-to-date equipment. Technical colleges and factory training schools are open to youngsters eager to learn the latest techniques.

The Chinese are well aware of their backwardness and they hope that

*Boatmen along the Yangtze River strain at their harness as they pull craft upstream.*

the use of humans as draft animals will soon be a thing of the past. Already in some of the larger cities the "pedicab"—a bicycle rickshaw—is being replaced by small taxis, tiny cars made for this purpose in Shanghai. But for all their efforts the Chinese have a long way to go before they become a fully modernized nation.

# BOOKSTALLS: THE NEW READERS

ALTHOUGH the Chinese invented printing and paper more than a thousand years ago, the country has had an astonishingly high rate of illiteracy up to the present century. The written language is difficult, employing thousands of complicated ideographs instead of a simple alphabet. Many village people who can read still must use a public letter writer for their correspondence. The proper formation of the characters is an art—words must be written with careful proportions and each line and stroke has to be done just so.

Since the 1920's the Chinese have been trying to solve the problem of illiteracy with a simplification of their language. The "Thousand Character System," a vocabulary of the most commonly used words, has been taught since World War I and has enabled people to learn to read simple texts in a matter of months, where formerly it took years. Now the government is making plans for an even more drastic short cut to literacy. Over the next ten years the Roman alphabet of twenty-six letters is going to be introduced, and the Chinese will learn to write their Mandarin dialect phonetically.

In a country the size of China there are numerous dialects as well as the languages of the minority groups, and communicating with masses that are multilingual is one of the tougher jobs confronting the government. Eventually it will have to insist that everyone learn Mandarin at school, though native dialects may still be spoken at home. Meanwhile, there are more people who can read in China today than there ever were before, thanks to the efforts made over the past forty years. So the demand for books has grown. First printings are often of fifty thousand copies, and some books go on to sell by the millions. Outdoor bookstalls like these in a public park are common. There is just one fly in the literary ointment. Some writers are becoming too successful, and there have been demands lately for best-selling authors to reduce their royalties voluntarily lest a new rich and privileged class develop.

# MOVIES: FIVE BILLION CUSTOMERS

**T**HOUGH China has always resisted Western influence, the country under the Communists is adopting many Western ways. Chinese ideographs are giving way to the Roman alphabet. Clothing, haircuts and sports have, like young Lochinvar, come out of the West. And mass production and movies are two cherished borrowings from our despised culture.

Here we see a film being made in one of Shanghai's newest movie studios. The ingredients are the same as in Hollywood—a pretty girl, a romantic leading man and a battery of klieg lights. "Lights! Camera! Action!"

The nation's burgeoning movie industry caters to audiences totaling more than five billion a year. There are key studios in at least four other cities, and movie theaters have mushroomed in many communities.

*In the traditional Chinese theater make-up is elaborate and actors strive for an unrealistic effect.*

Where they don't exist, mobile projection units travel to communes, factories and out-of-the-way villages to show the latest movies. Chinese pictures extol the advantages of the Communist system, the need for more production and, of course, the wisdom and kindness of the leaders (whose government controls the industry). But the propaganda does not seem to deter the hardy Chinese moviegoers who patiently sit through such films as *In Praise of Heroes, New Story of an Old Soldier,* and *Lads and Lasses of Our Village.* No bingo, no free China, either.

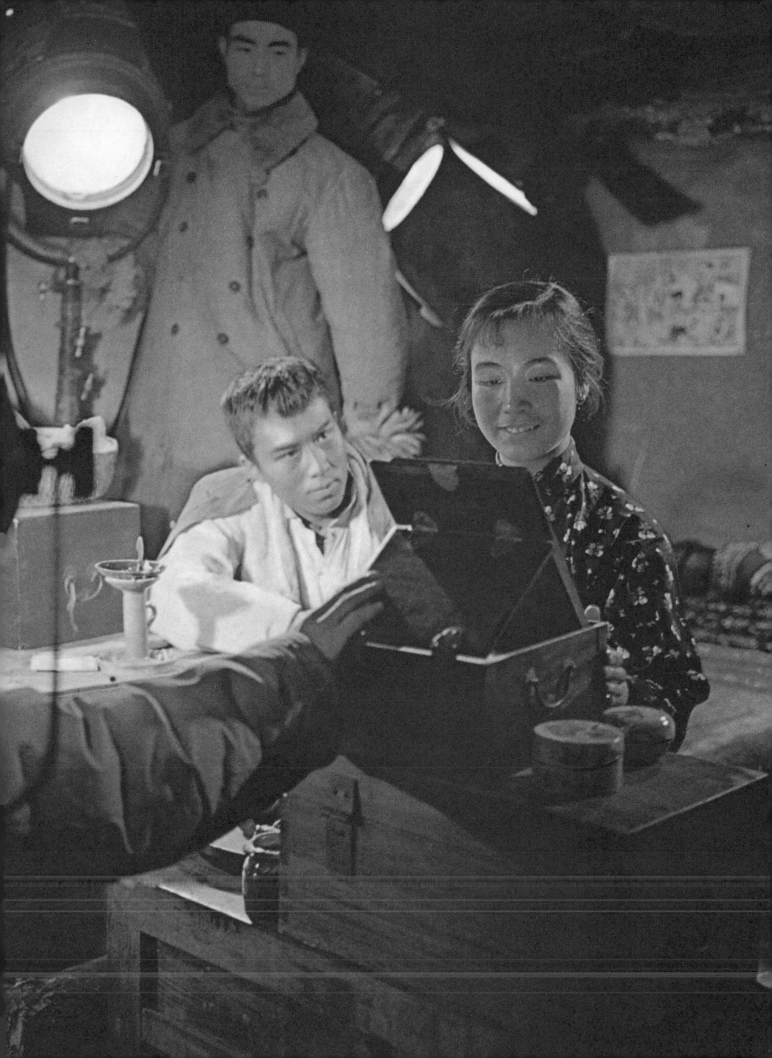

# SHANGHAI: OLD TREATY PORT

A CHINESE junk with bat-wing sails all but obliterates our view of the once thriving waterfront of Shanghai. In the old days this was one of the great seaports of the world, and ships from every major country used to dock at its wharves on the Hwang Pu (*hwahng poo*) branch of the Yangtze River. Of all the cities in China, Shanghai, Queen of the China Coast, was the best-known to Westerners, and it still retains a cosmopolitan flavor. The tall hotels and stately commercial palaces, built by Europeans when Shanghai was a treaty port, stand at the river's edge and give the city a most un-Chinese skyline. Sampans, a few junks, an occasional freighter drift across the expanse of water where formerly as many as thirty ocean-going ships docked each day.

Shanghai is built on the flat rich delta of the Yangtze River, China's main artery of water traffic. Large ships can travel up the river to Hankow, 690 miles away, and junks and steamboats can navigate the treacherous Yangtze beyond Chungking, to a point about 1800 miles from the river's mouth. Today Shanghai has a population of six and a half million and is an important industrial and commercial center. The International Settlement is gone, the night life of a welcoming seaport has been eradicated and parts of the city have been cleaned up. But there is an afterglow of Shanghai's fascinating past in the neon lights, the brighter clothes and the few remaining Chinese millionaires (industrialists useful to the present regime), that sets this city apart from all the others.

# DAIREN: INDUSTRIAL MANCHURIA

**D**AIREN (*dye-ren*), which the Chinese call Talien (*tah-lyen*), is one of China's largest seaports, with easy access to the Pacific via the Yellow Sea. Lying far to the northeast in Manchuria (a name the Chinese never use, although it was the homeland of their Manchu rulers), Dairen is indicative of the industrial activity of this area. Coal and water power have made Manchuria a valuable industrial region, forests in the eastern highlands provide China with her largest timber reserves, and the soils of the Manchurian plain are deep and fertile.

Russia and Japan have been trying to control Manchuria for decades, and in World War II it was occupied by the Japanese. Soviet troops ousted the Japanese in 1945, and the Russian forces in turn withdrew one year later. But they withdrew with them nearly every piece of industrial equipment that wasn't nailed down tight. According to the Pauley report, the equipment removed by Russia had a replacement value of two billion dollars.

Chinese Communists got a foothold in Manchuria, and by 1948 this was the first region to come completely under Communist domination. Since 1949 the Soviet has been supplying Red China with aid in Manchuria in the form of technical help, modest loans and the sale of dismantled factories. Much of the industrial equipment, carried by Russian freighters like the one in this picture, has come through the ice-free port of Dairen to this region that is the mainspring of China's industrial development. The steel cranes silhouetted against Manchuria's cold blue skies are perhaps more significant to China and the rest of the world than the red banners that fly in Peking.

# STEEL MILL:
# CHINA'S
# SINEWS

A VISIT to a steel mill is not, in other countries, usually considered a tourist attraction. But in Red China the grim and charmless industrial landscape of Manchuria and the roaring, smoky factories and mills are showplaces to be exhibited with pride. As we trudge through the dust and fiery glare of this steel mill, our guide—always a good Party member—will give us a running commentary, complete with elaborate figures, to show how much has been achieved under Communism. The people who are chosen to speak to foreign visitors tend to sound as though they had swallowed an official brochure.

There is no way to check the accuracy of the guide's statistics and figures, but the plants, the factories, the generating stations, the coal mines are there to be seen, either recently completed or still under construction. The Anshan Steel Company, now State-owned, was in ruins when it was taken over by the Chinese Communists in 1949. But the Peking government concentrated on restoring and expanding heavy industry and, with the help of Soviet technicians, industrial development made great strides. Agriculture has not kept pace with industry, but a steel mill, like the one at Anshan, can at least feed national pride.

*The face of new China peers from the protective headpiece of a factory worker.*

41

# BUILDING
# EVERYWHERE:
# RURAL
# HOUSING

EVERYWHERE we travel in China we see buildings in the process of construction. There is a feverish drive to meet the urgent need for new factories, schools, hospitals, clinics, libraries, public halls—and, of course, houses. Newly established colleges of architecture send out teachers and students to rural areas to help the peasants build. Here we watch the construction of some new rural houses for peasants. The methods are rather rough-and-ready—many of the workers have never done this work before —but the houses are invariably of brick, sturdy and constructed with incredible rapidity.

While much of the rural construction is of poor design, large public buildings constructed in the cities aim at some sort of style. Chinese architects have attempted to combine traditional designs with modern construction, and many of them, in spite of Marxist indoctrination, have included the ancient figures and symbols used for centuries to ward off evil spirits from a Chinese building. The Great Hall of the People in Peking was designed, built, landscaped and equipped in ten months. It has an auditorium that seats ten thousand people under a domed ceiling decorated with the red star of Communism. It remains to be seen whether this talisman is any luckier than the ancient Chinese figures.

*Behind flimsy bamboo scaffolding a modern building—the central telegraph office—goes up in Peking.*

# GRINDING CORN: THE GOOD EARTH

ON MANY of the small farms in China, scenes such as this are not uncommon. This woman is grinding corn on a primitive stone wheel. She symbolizes the endless labor of China's millions of peasants, for this farm could be anywhere in China, and could be now or a thousand years ago. From time immemorial the life of the Chinese peasant has been dominated by the struggle for the basic necessities of life. It would be a mistake, however, to suppose that the peasants are a sullen or unhappy people. Their manners are gentle, and even in great poverty they retain a certain buoyancy and humor. Close to the soil that sustains them, they live in harmony with the rhythms of nature . . . the changing seasons . . . sowing and harvest . . . birth and death.

One of the great unifying factors in the four thousand years of Chinese civilization has been the family system. In rural China this meant that clan villages were the usual communities, made up of one family with its various branches. However simple the ancestral home was, it had a series of courts with surrounding rooms, and a community threshing floor, water supply, vegetable garden and burial ground. There was no need of poorhouses, orphanages, insane asylums or even insurance companies. Each clan took care of its own, so that even in poverty there was security, and everyone knew he had a place where he would be welcome and cared for.

The fabric of family life that had been tough enough to endure for thousands of years began to disintegrate in this century. Industrialization and the dislocation of people during invasions and war began the process. The Communist regime has taken large numbers of women into industry, disrupting millions of homes. Today the commune is supplanting the clan, and household tasks are handled by communal kitchens, nurseries and laundries. The old values have been destroyed but the endless work goes on.

# CHINESE FOOD: CULINARY ART

**T**HOSE of us who pride ourselves on a taste for Chinese food quickly discover when we come to China that there is a much wider variety than we had imagined. We are standing now in the vegetable market in Tientsin (*tyen-tsin*) and it is vegetables such as these that form a major part of the Chinese diet. Preparation and taste differ greatly, however, from region to region.

Food in southwest China is as peppery and fiery hot as anything found in Mexico. North Chinese dishes are often highly flavored with garlic, and there—as a result of Moslem influence—much mutton is eaten. A small caldron is often set on the table in a restaurant and the diners dip small pieces of mutton into the boiling water with chopsticks. And no meal, of course, anywhere in China is complete without many cups of tea. For visitors to China one of the delights is to discover the out-of-the-way restaurants (often quite small), but most Chinese would be able to eat in a restaurant only as a rare treat.

We discover that rice is not eaten as a staple throughout China, but mostly in the south. Wheat and millets are more common in the north. The Chinese are becoming great beer drinkers, but rice wine—sometimes served hot—is still a favorite.

*Steaming soup, sold by a street vendor, is served in delicate porcelain.*

# FOUR-LEGGED CROP: MEAT FOR THE MILLIONS

**W**HEREVER we travel in the Chinese countryside, we are conscious of the never-ending struggle to produce more food for the huge population. Pork is the main meat in the Chinese diet (except for China's ten million Moslems)—but it is not often that the average peasant enjoys it. In some areas the peasants eat meat only on festival days, perhaps six times a year, but foreign visitors are wined and dined sumptuously. Today, throughout China, there is a national "pig drive" to encourage the peasants to raise more pigs.

Although the communes have promised rapid changes, we still see everywhere farming methods that have been handed down from ancient days, many of them pathetically inadequate. As China's industries develop, modern agricultural methods are being introduced. But the periodic famines that have shadowed all the centuries of Chinese history occur even in this century of technological advances.

Small workshops have now been set up in all the villages of China—hundreds of thousands of them. Here the peasants work when they are not busy in the fields. They make all kinds of machine parts needed by Chinese industries, as well as radio sets and other electronic apparatus, but this versatility does not fill bare cupboards.

*Water pumps worked by foot power are used to flood rice fields in the age-old way.*

# WORK
# AND LEARN:
# EVERYONE'S
# JOB

WATCHING these men dig out an old canal by hand—a job we would perform with a single bulldozer—we realize that China makes do with sheer manpower when there are no machines. Human muscles and sinews have always done most of the work in China, from planting and irrigating the fields to building railroads, bridges and dams. In the cities pedicabs and peditrucks—vehicles propelled by manpower—are being abolished because the government says it is not dignified for humans to act as beasts of burden. But beyond the city limits this tender regard for human dignity gives way to the necessity for getting things done.

Along the railways you see gangs of men and women, sometimes by the thousands, working with picks and shovels to widen the roadbeds, and carrying baskets of earth and gravel to be dumped elsewhere. There is an old saying, "Make them tired and you will keep them happy." Certainly the leaders of Red China seem to be following that principle.

For millions of Chinese the end of an eight-hour day in factory or field is only the beginning of a new day—in which they go to a "spare-time school" or to a political instruction class. Almost every Chinese must attend classes in Marxist doctrine at least once, and often twice, each week. In these meetings the works of Lenin and Mao Tse-tung are read and discussed and the behavior of the members of the discussion groups is often brought up for criticism or praise. Spare time is further occupied with campaigns to clean up China, get rid of flies and pests, abolish illiteracy and increase production. On Sundays there are occasional parades, and so full a schedule leaves no time or energy for discontent. There are only about thirteen million members of the Communist Party in China, but it is to these young "cadres" or leaders that the government looks to see that instructions are carried out at the local level, and that everyone keeps working and learning.

50

# WOMEN WORKERS: COMMUNE FARMING

SOME of the hardest, most backbreaking jobs in China are done by women. They clean the streets, work in steel mills, operate streetcars, dynamite rocks for road building, serve in the army, row cargo sampans and labor in the fields. As a result of their new legal equality with men they wear the same clothes—blue trousers and shirts, hold the same jobs and are sometimes difficult to recognize as women. The only thing women still may not do is play female parts on the stage—they never were allowed to.

The sheer grind of hard work has not been lifted from women's shoulders, for they constitute about thirty per cent of Red China's labor power. But compared with the days when female babies were sometimes drowned, and women had neither property nor rights and were little more than slaves in their husband's house, the new "freedom" seems to live up to its name.

In factories and on farms you see men and women working side by side. The girls wear their hair either in the short, square-cut bob popularized by the women of the People's Army, or in more modish pigtails. In either case, and thanks to the sternly unalluring clothes they wear, they are no distraction for their male colleagues. In communes the workers live in dormitories, or in single-room accommodations for families. Close to the factories or fields there are nurseries for the youngest children, and mothers may leave their work at intervals to nurse their babies. These people, once so firmly cemented into families, enjoy little family life these days. They don't even refer to their living places as homes or apartments, but instead use the more institutional term, dormitory. They are fed from a community kitchen where the food, though simple, is usually adequate. By the coolie standards of Red China this is considered the good life, and as yet only a fraction of the huge population has attained it.

# APPLE SELLER: PRIVATE ENTERPRISE

IN SOME of the larger cities of Red China private enterprise still exists in back-street bazaars or sidewalk markets. Here produce from private gardens is for sale, and soups and other dishes are cooked to order in little outdoor stalls. Generally the vendors are old Chinese who have not been educated to the new way of doing things. In a city like Peking these last practitioners of capitalism are a colorful crew. Many of them operate pushcarts from which they sell spices, chestnuts, tidbits of cooked meat, household goods, goldfish, songbirds and even stringed instruments.

In the old days the peddlers announced their wares with singsong chants and instruments that were identified with their products. The melon-seed vendors beat a special brass gong; the thump of a leather drum meant a cloth seller was coming up the street; the clanging of two brass bowls introduced the peddler with his tray of dried fruit and nuts;

*A peddler walks along the streets of Peking, chanting his sales talk as he goes.*

while the itinerant barber made himself known by pinging a tuning fork. These sounds still add to the din of Peking, only now they must compete with the racket of numerous loud-speakers spotted along the streets. The amplifiers blare martial music and shout propaganda tirelessly all day long. But the old capitalist in our picture doesn't seem to mind. She sits in the winter sunshine behind her meager display of privately owned apples and keeps her fur earflaps down.

# YELLOW RIVER DAM: TAMING "CHINA'S SORROW"

THE Yellow River, or Hwang Ho, loops across northwest China for a distance of 2700 miles. Much of the land it traverses is arid, and the river gets its name from the yellow earth it picks up and carries in enormous quantities to the Yellow Sea. The Hwang Ho is an unpredictable river. In some places its opaque water rushes in torrents, in others it moves sluggishly in a broad channel. At certain seasons it overflows and the north China plain is devasted with floods. Furthermore, the river changes its course occasionally with disastrous effects both in destruction of farm lands and loss of life.

The population is extremely dense in the fertile land along the Yellow River, but because of the frequent flooding, millions live in peril. One million people perished in its floods in one year. Control of the Hwang Ho has been a problem the Chinese have tried to solve for centuries. In many places dikes have been built and the river channel modified. Now the government has a vast project going and it hopes that by harnessing the Yellow River, "China's Sorrow" will become "China's Joy."

Along the riverbanks armies of men and women, clad in the inevitable blue, swarm along newly built roads carrying baskets of dirt or crushed rock. Concrete factories have been set up on both shores, and ant-like blue throngs are in constant motion, building bridges, pouring concrete, raising a giant dam to hold the swirling muddy water. In this picture we see the construction gang at work, and notice with some surprise that there are long braids hanging from the helmet of one of the workers. It is strange to think that this girl in rough workman's shoes is a descendant of the delicate Chinese women who minced along on bound feet just a few generations ago.

# THE GREAT WALL: HISTORIC RAMPART

THE most ambitious engineering feat of ancient times was the Great Wall of China. In the north a number of warring kingdoms had built walls as a defense against one another and to keep out the northern nomads. Then, twenty-two hundred years ago, the first emperor of the Ch'in (*chin*) dynasty (which gave China its name) linked some of the older walls to make a continuous rampart. The Great Wall climbs over steep mountains and wanders over distant deserts. It snakes across north China for two thousand miles, from the sea westward to the edge of the Tibetan plateau. In the old days it separated the settled agricultural people of China from the wanderers of the steppe.

Primarily the Wall was built as a military defense, but it failed in its purpose. It was breached many times by invaders who found it simpler to bribe the gatekeepers than to attack the fortification. Over the centuries there were changes in climate which changed the old boundary marked by the Wall. There were times when grazing land became desert, forcing nomads to migrate southward. There were other times when the grasslands beyond the Wall became moist enough for cultivation, and Chinese farmers moved outside its confines.

The Great Wall remains today as one of the marvels of Old China. To see it, you can drive about forty miles north of Peking to a spot where the Wall has been fully restored. The north wind, whipping down from Siberia and Mongolia, batters against the Wall, which is no more effective against it than it was against other northern invaders. The Great Wall represents China's past determination to keep out all foreign influence, all "barbarians" from other lands. Yet within this vast country there are many peoples, and the former national flag, created after the 1911 Revolution, recognized these multiple races. It had five stripes: yellow for the Han (or Chinese proper), red for the Manchus, white for the Mohammedans, blue for Mongols and black for Tibetans.

58

# TIBETAN WOMEN: THE MOUNTAIN PEOPLE

REMOTE and inaccessible, the high tableland of Tibet is one of the most fascinating regions in the world. Under Manchu rule it was part of the Chinese Empire, but when the dynasty was overthrown, Tibet asserted its independence. The Communists invaded it in 1950, and nine years later when the Tibetan religious and government leader, the Dalai Lama, fled to India, the Communists went to work in earnest to institute social changes in Tibet. Young Tibetans are being educated as political leaders in a number of Institutes of National Minorities that have been set up in Red China. But the traditional aloofness of these people and their ancient way of life still keep them apart and distinct from the rest of the Chinese.

The Tibetan plateau is about fifteen thousand feet above sea level, with mountain peaks towering five or ten thousand feet higher. It is a bleak land, but the people who inhabit it are colorful. These Tibetan women wear the typical long, full gown, padded with cotton or lined with lambskin to protect them from the bitter cold. The gowns are tied tightly around the waist, then bloused above it. The pouch that results is used for carrying odds and ends—a drinking cup, utensils or something to amuse the baby.

All male children, whether from peasant families or the nobility, have an equal chance of glory. The Tibetans believe that their highest Buddhist monks, or lamas, are reborn, and they have certain indications to tell them which little boys are "incarnations." Sometimes even the Dalai Lama, the highest monk of all, is reborn as a baby in a lowly family. When that happens the family is ennobled and given large estates. As long as the belief in incarnation exists, every red-cheeked little Tibetan boy is a potential lama. Not that that has anything at all to do with the typical expressions of maternal pride we see in this picture.

# NORTHERN WINTER: LONG, COLD SEASON

THE people who inhabit the highlands of Tibet have a cold climate all year round, but the rest of China has extreme seasonal variations. The south, which is greener and more fertile, enjoys a long summer with growing time for several crops. The dry, brown north has a short but hot summer and a winter that lingers, keeping the fields barren for many months of the year.

You will see the Chinese bundled up against the biting cold in thickly padded garments. The men and women wear somber black or dark blue, but children are usually dressed in vivid colors that set off their dark eyes and olive skin. The Chinese say that a toddler who is ready to learn to walk in wintertime has to wait until summer. His bulky garments, which he wears indoors too, make it impossible for him to move his limbs and balance properly. Frequently you see children, like the one in this picture, slip and fall on the icy ground. Then an adult must run to pick up the well-wrapped bundle and set it on its feet again.

In the heat of summer, even as far north as Peking, children wear only the skimpiest of attire, and boys under four years of age usually wear nothing at all. As for the adults, when you see them in their lightweight garments after the long winter is over, they all seem to have become smaller and very much thinner.

*Mud-walled houses are unheated, but when families can spend their days together the atmosphere is warm and cozy.*

62

# OLD GENERATION: TIES WITH THE PAST

**M**ANY of the Chinese people still live very close to their past, materially and spiritually. This old man sunning himself outside the once restricted Forbidden City in Peking has, in his lifetime, seen the Manchu dynasty, the war lords, floods, famine, foreign invasion, civil war—and now a Communist government. And he may well be thinking that Communism, too, may pass and be remembered as merely another turbulent "episode" in China's immortal history.

Many of the older people have been caught up in the drive to industrialize the nation. The need for labor is so demanding that age is no barrier to employment—there is work for everyone according to his capacity. Some of the "Heroes of Labor" cited by the government are men and women well in their fifties. It is possible that these older people had been "educated" by their children about proper attitudes toward work. Filial piety has undergone some changes in this new society. Red China encourages youngsters to report their parents to the police if they seem laggard in fulfilling their duties to the State.

But in spite of this new order, among many Chinese the elderly still retain their place of honor and respect. And if this old man should climb onto a crowded bus, some younger person would immediately rise to give him a seat. Like people everywhere, most of the humble people of China are concerned not with political theories and shouted slogans, but —as they have been through the ages—with the very simple realities and problems and joys of daily life. They take their pleasures as and when they come, and to sit in the sun is good while it lasts.

# PHYSICAL
# FITNESS:
# THE DAILY
# DOZEN

CHINA'S new rulers place great importance on physical culture, and since 1949 they have spent large sums of money for stadiums, gymnasiums and swimming pools. By government decree China is being made sports-conscious, and twice a day there is an exercise break when loud-speakers exhort people in shops, offices and schools to drop everything for ten minutes of calisthenics. It is one of the odder sights in Red China to see a crew of maintenance men and scrubwomen leave their back-breaking jobs for a session of exercise to music.

The little boy in this picture is performing calisthenics known as *T'ai-chi ch'üan*. Each stylized movement is dictated by tradition, for this series of exercises is very ancient. Harmony and grace, those virtues prized so highly by the old Chinese, were achieved as a result of practicing *T'ai-chi ch'üan*. The exercises are done in slow motion, and perfect balance must be maintained while different muscles are flexed and the performer shifts from one ballet-like position to another. Formerly only older men went through this exacting drill, but now these traditional calisthenics have become popular with young people too.

The Communists' insistence upon physical fitness is understandable in the light of their dependency upon manpower to achieve for them what other countries can do with machines. "Train for ten minutes every day," they tell their people, "and you'll be able to serve the cause of socialism for ten additional years." The fitness and exercise program is aimed especially at intellectuals; Chinese workers who lift and strain, pull and carry from sunup to sundown are hardly in need of additional exercise. But in the past, scholars and intellectuals scorned physical work. Today even college classes are interrupted for setting-up exercises, and sports are being encouraged as never before. If a school or institute lacks a playground, its members have to get into condition by going out with shovels and baskets and making one.

# MASS EDUCATION: THE TWO R'S

ANY government that intends to maintain itself in power with a centralized authoritarian administration must be able to communicate with the people; and for this the people need to be able to read and write. Consequently the Chinese Communists have given a very high priority to that aspect of education. You might say that schooling is compulsory in China, except for the fact that there are not yet enough buildings and teachers to accommodate the millions of students—willing or unwilling—who are ready for school.

It is difficult to know what the exact statistics are, but certainly there are more children being educated in China today than ever before. In the primary schools they are being taught to read and write, thus ensuring an audience that can understand what the government wants of it. Secondary and high schools have been lagging, and they are not supplying enough graduates to fill available places in the universities. The children in this picture are at a school attached to their city commune. They may never have the opportunity to learn the great Chinese classics that are their true heritage, but they will at least have the tools to understand them, should the future ever bring them into contact with their country's illustrious past.

*These schoolgirls have much to learn from the elderly Chinese who has mastered an ancient system of exercise.*

# STREET IN
# TAIPEI:
# NATIONALIST
# CAPITAL

SHARING the cultural heritage of Red China but following a different political course, the Republic of China has been set up on Taiwan and its neighboring islands, less than a hundred miles from the mainland. In the sixteenth century, Portuguese sailors sighted the green peaks of the island and named it Formosa—beautiful. But the Chinese and Japanese have always called it Taiwan. The Japanese governed the island from 1895 until 1945, and it was a profitable colony, supplying rice and sugar to Japan as well as profits from exports such as tea. In 1945 Taiwan was returned to China as a province. In 1949 the Nationalist Government moved its capital to Taipei (*tie-pay*), the largest city on the island, and the population of Taiwan was swelled by an influx of mainlanders and people connected with the government, plus half a million soldiers.

The Chinese Republic, founded after the fall of the Manchus in 1912, was largely the creation of the revolutionary leader Dr. Sun Yat-sen. In 1923 Sun accepted help from Russia in holding his government together, and admitted the Communist party into the Nationalist movement. After Sun's death, Chiang Kai-shek broke with the Communists and booted them out of the government. The Republic of China, which Chiang heads here in Taiwan, is based on the original principles of Sun Yat-sen's republic, and its primary aim is to recover the rest of China from the Communists.

On the streets of Taipei, a city of 800,000, certain differences between the two Chinas are apparent at once. Most obvious is the brightness and variety of the people's clothing. The regulation blue boiler-room suits of Red China have given way to individualized attire. Movies are a popular form of entertainment here, and a number of the films are American. The United States has given military and economic aid to the Republic of China, and considerable progress has been made in the past decade. But Taiwan, which is one of the most densely populated areas in the world, will find it difficult to become self-supporting.

70

# TEA HARVESTERS: GIRLS OF TAIWAN

**T**HE tea known as Formosa oolong is world-famous and the girls who harvest it fit the old Portuguese description of their island. On the hillsides of northern Taiwan, about 100,000 acres are devoted to the growing of tea. The leaves are prepared in three different ways. Green tea is dried rapidly so that very little fermentation takes place. The brown or amber oolong variety, Taiwan's chief export to the United States, is allowed to ferment partially during processing. When it is flavored with jasmine or gardenia it makes a delicate and fragrant brew. Black tea is made when the drying of the leaves is delayed so that full fermentation and oxidation take place. In 1958 more than thirty million pounds of tea were produced on the terraced hillsides, picked by girls like these.

In spite of the highly touted "new freedom" of Red China's women, they are a fairly grim-looking lot compared with their sisters on Taiwan. The influences of the twentieth century and Western attitudes toward women have reached Taiwan, too, and these girls manage to look pretty and feminine even in their work clothes. Taiwan is predominantly agricultural, and there have been recent land reforms that redistributed holdings and resulted in increased efficiency.

*Tea is blended in Taiwan for export. Then it is tested in the time-honored way— by tasting a cupful.*

# MING TOMB: IMPERIAL MONUMENT

THOUGH at present China is divided politically, the people in both camps have centuries of civilization and history in common. The leaders of Red China seem to be facing in a new direction, yet they encourage a backward glance at the past by carefully preserving its matchless monuments. Here we are at a popular sight-seeing spot twenty-five miles northwest of Peking. This is the Valley of the Tombs, where thirteen Ming emperors were buried from the fourteenth to the seventeenth centuries. Surrounded by rolling purple hills, these famous tombs are scattered in a wide half-circle that fans out for thirty miles.

The road leading to the site is lined with exotic marble beasts, Ming sculptures on a grand scale. The courtyards are enclosed within crimson walls, and the shrines have had their vivid colors restored. Some of the buildings are massive, and hundreds of years ago gigantic teakwood columns and blocks of pink marble were dragged by men all the way from Yunnan, in southern China, for their construction. In two magnificent exhibition halls are displayed the brocaded robes, the exquisite gold dragon crown, the jade and gold articles that were found here. This splendor was created by the labor and skill of the Chinese who lived and toiled under the Ming emperors.

Today's leaders, while decrying "imperialistic exploitation," are creating their new projects by much the same means. The Ming Tombs Reservoir nearby was built by 400,000 "volunteers" brought out from Peking by the busload. The huge earth dam was raised in 1958 as a result of the efforts of those thousands of Chinese. They scraped earth from the surrounding hills, and carried it basketful by basketful to the dam site. The imagination is staggered at the thought of the man-hours that went into both of these grandiose projects, and the feeling that essentially methods have changed little in China from Ming to Mao.

# PEKING OPERA: DISTURBANCE IN HEAVEN

FOR ten centuries the Chinese have been addicted to their noisy, gaudy, intricate and brilliant classical opera. Wherever Chinese have settled—in Singapore, Hong Kong, Manila and Taiwan, as well as in Red China itself—the beloved characters and traditional plays can be seen. Within the walls of the theater the outside world is forgotten, and only the action on the stage exists. A single opera can last five hours, and the audience lives every minute of it with passionate intensity.

In the eighteenth century this form of theater reached the imperial court at Peking and it has been called "Peking Opera" ever since. To Western ears it is a far loud cry from opera. Cymbals clash, gongs boom, drums thunder, and a welter of noise splits the air. The actors strut and prance in fantastic make-up and costumes. And the clowning and acrobatics are magnificently performed. Here we see one of the most popular operatic characters, the Monkey King, busily eating a sacred peach in the opera *Disturbance in Heaven*. This character, a rebel against authority who triumphs over evil gods and spirits, has been cavorting across Chinese stages for centuries. Thus far the authorities have let classical opera alone, and have turned their propaganda efforts to Chinese drama, or "dialogue plays" instead.

*Students learn the national dances of other countries as well as Western classical ballet.*

# OUTDOOR AUDIENCE: THE FACES OF CHINA

**T**HIS is the audience, at least as interesting as the performers, at a traveling show of the Peking Opera. Reflected in their animated faces is the action—melodramatic, broadly humorous—which has aroused emotion in generations of Chinese. The theater has been an important part of Chinese life all through recorded history and it is really the national pastime. On the average, three million persons see some sort of play or opera in China each day!

These people, serious-looking or impassive when they face the realities of life in the new China, are utterly transformed by the make-believe of the stage. We glimpse them here for a moment, carried out of themselves by a Monkey King's mischief, an emperor's wrath or a war lord's ferocity. These same plays have been performed through the

*Refugees from Red China wait wearily to cross the frontier where the British flag waves over Hong Kong.*

centuries — under good emperors and bad, strong rulers and weak, foreign oppressors and home-grown tyrants. The gongs beat furiously and the deafening noise shuts out the world. For a few hours the Chinese audience finds escape in a changeless old art.

78

# SOME IMPORTANT DATES IN CHINESE HISTORY

c. 3,000 B.C. — *Origins of present-day Chinese people and culture in the Yellow River area.*

255-206 B.C. — *Ch'in dynasty. Unification of China under the first emperor. Great Wall is completed.*

c. 202 B.C.-220 A.D. — *Han dynasty. Invention of paper and seismograph.*

618-907 — *T'ang dynasty. Period of China's greatest poets—Li Po, Tu Fu and Po Chü-i. Printing is invented.*

960-1280 — *Sung dynasty. Invention of movable type and the cannon. A period of great art. Start of the Mongol invasion.*

1368-1644 — *Following the driving out of Mongols, Ming dynasty rules China. Arrival of Jesuit missionaries and European ships. Manchus breach the Great Wall, and assume power.*

1793 — *Manchu government turns down British request to open China to trade with West.*

1839-1842 — *First Opium War. Britain forces China to cede Hong Kong to Britain and grant rights of residence and trade to foreigners in five treaty ports.*

1850-1865 — *T'ai P'ing Rebellion against emperor, begun by a fanatical religious sect, causes enormous loss of life.*

1856-1860 — *Second foreign war. China, defeated again, opens the interior to outsiders, accepts missionary activity and grants extraterritoriality, or exemption from local law, to European settlements.*

1894-1895 — *Sino-Japanese War ends in China's defeat.*

1899-1900 — *Boxer Rebellion against the "foreign devils." European, American, Japanese forces relieve the siege of Peking.*

1911-1912 — *Overthrow of Manchu dynasty and founding of the Republic, which attempts unsuccessfully to modernize nation.*

1919 — *"May 4th Movement" protesting Treaty of Versailles which gave territory in Shantung Province to Japan.*

1921 — *Communist Party formed. Kuomintang (Nationalists) and Communists ally in 1923 to fight war lords and create a united China capable of resisting encroachment of its sovereignty.*

1927 — *Split between Kuomintang and Communists brings civil war.*

1931 — *Manchuria (Northeast China) invaded by Japanese; puppet state of Manchukuo set up.*

1937 — *Kuomintang, under Chiang Kai-shek, and Communists, under Mao Tse-tung, agree to end civil war and resist Japanese.*

1945 — *War ends with Japanese defeat by Western powers.*

1946 — *Civil war resumes. Forces of Chiang Kai-shek are defeated. Communists set up government in Peking, October 1st, 1949.*

1950 — *Communist Chinese troops enter North Korea against United Nations forces.*

1953 — *United States and Red China sign armistice ending United Nations police action in Korea.*

1958 — *Communes are established throughout Red China.*

# SOME FAMOUS NAMES IN CHINESE HISTORY

**CONFUCIUS (c. 551-479 B.C.)**—*Ancient China's greatest scholar. His philosophy, based on proper rules of conduct, has profoundly influenced Chinese society.*

**CHU YUAN (340-278 B.C.)**—*First of China's many great poets, also a great statesman. His death is still celebrated on the fifth day of the fifth moon.*

**SSU-MA CH'IEN (145?-87 B.C.)**—*First great historian of China. In more than 500,000 words he recorded 2,000 years of Chinese history.*

**TSU CHUNG-CHIH (429-500)**—*Scientist and student of mathematics and astronomy. His figure of 3.14159265 for pi was the most precise in the world in his day.*

**T'AI TSUNG (597-649)**—*Second T'ang emperor, who began the system of civil service examinations. The first Christian missionaries arrived during his reign.*

**LI PO (?-762)**—*Widely regarded as China's greatest poet. He lived a dissipated life at court and drowned in a tipsy attempt to embrace the moon reflected in a river.*

**WANG AN-SHIH (1021-1086)**—*Prime Minister of Sung dynasty. Noted for numerous reforms, including vast irrigation works and aid for tenant farmers.*

**GENGHIS KHAN (1162-1227)**—*Mongol emperor who conquered virtually all of China and Central Asia. His forces advanced as far as the Danube in Europe.*

**MARCO POLO (c. 1254-1324)**—*Famous Venetian who journeyed to China and returned with reports of the fabulous empire of Kublai Khan, grandson of Genghis.*

**LI SHIH-CHEN (1518-1593)**—*Outstanding medical researcher and author of numerous works dealing with the science of medicine.*

**LIN TSE-HSU (1785-1850)**—*Viceroy appointed by emperor to ban opium imports by British in Canton. Confiscated more than 20,000 chests of opium, thereby leading events to first Opium War.*

**SUN YAT-SEN (1866-1925)**—*Chinese statesman and patriot who led revolution against Manchu rule which established the first Republic of China.*

**LU HSUN (1881-1936)**—*Leading writer of the twentieth century, a member of Sun Yat-sen's political movement.*

**CHIANG KAI-SHEK (1886-     )**—*Military and political leader of Nationalist Party after Sun Yat-sen's death. President of the Republic of China on the island of Taiwan.*

**MAO TSE-TUNG (1893-     )**—*Politician and poet. Chairman and leading member of the Chinese Communist Party for more than three decades.*

**CHOU EN-LAI (1898?-     )**—*One of the founders of the Chinese Communist Party, and first premier of the People's Republic of China.*

# SOME CHINESE WORDS AND PHRASES

Here is a list of words and phrases that you might be likely to use when traveling in China. They are translated first into the English equivalent of the Chinese characters and this is followed by a simple phonetic pronunciation. The Chinese language also relies heavily on the use of varying tonal qualities, which we have not attempted to indicate in this vocabulary.

| | |
|---|---|
| How are you? | Ni hao (*nee how*) |
| Yes. | Shih (*shirh*) |
| No. | Pu shih (*boo shirh*) |
| Please. | Ch'ing (*cheeng*) |
| Excuse me. | Debuchi (*deh-boo-chee*) |
| Thank you. | Hsieh-hsieh ni (*shee-shee nee*) |
| Don't mention it. | Pu kang tang (*boo kahng dahng*) |
| What time is it? | Chi tien chung (*chee dee-en joong*) |
| I want to buy . . . | Wo yao mai . . . (*woh yah-oo my*) |
| Happy New Year! | Kung-hsi, kung-hsi (*goon-she goon-she*) |
| Do you speak English? | Ni huei shuo Ing-guo-hua ma (*nee hway shwor ying-gwor-hwah ma*) |
| Just a moment. | Teng i huei-erh (*tung ee hweh-erh*) |
| Where is the airport? | Fee-jee-chong tsai na-li (*fay-jee-chahng tsigh nah-lee*) |
| Good-bye. | Tsai chien (*tsigh jen*) |
| Restaurant | Fan kuan (*fon gwahn*) |
| Hotel | Lu kuan (*lew gwahn*) |
| Barber shop | Li-fa shih (*lee-fa shih*) |

## FOOD AND DRINK

| | |
|---|---|
| Food | Fan (*fon*) |
| Tea | Ch'a (*chah*) |
| Rice (cooked) | Pai fan (*by fon*) |
| Pork | Chu jou (*choo roh*) |
| Beef | Niu jou (*nyoo-roh*) |
| Chicken | Chi (*chee*) |
| Duck | Ya-tze (*yah-tsuh*) |
| Eggs | Chi-tan (*jee-don*) |
| Fish | Yu (*yew*) |
| Apples | P'ing kuo (*ping gwar*) |
| Grapes | P'u t'ao (*poo tah-oo*) |
| Rice wine | Huang-chiu (*hwahng-chew*) |

## NUMBERS

| | |
|---|---|
| One | i (*ee*) |
| Two | erh (*er*) |
| Three | san (*sahn*) |
| Four | sze (*tsuh*) |
| Five | wu (*woo*) |
| Six | liu (*lyou*) |
| Seven | chi (*chee*) |
| Eight | ba (*bah*) |
| Nine | ju (*jew*) |
| Ten | shih (*shirh*) |
| One hundred | i pai (*ee pie*) |
| One thousand | i chien (*ee chee-en*) |

## MONEY

Yuen (*yew-en*)
Mao (*mah-oo*)  Ten mao equals one yuen
Fen (*fen*)  One hundred fen equals one yuen

## INDEX